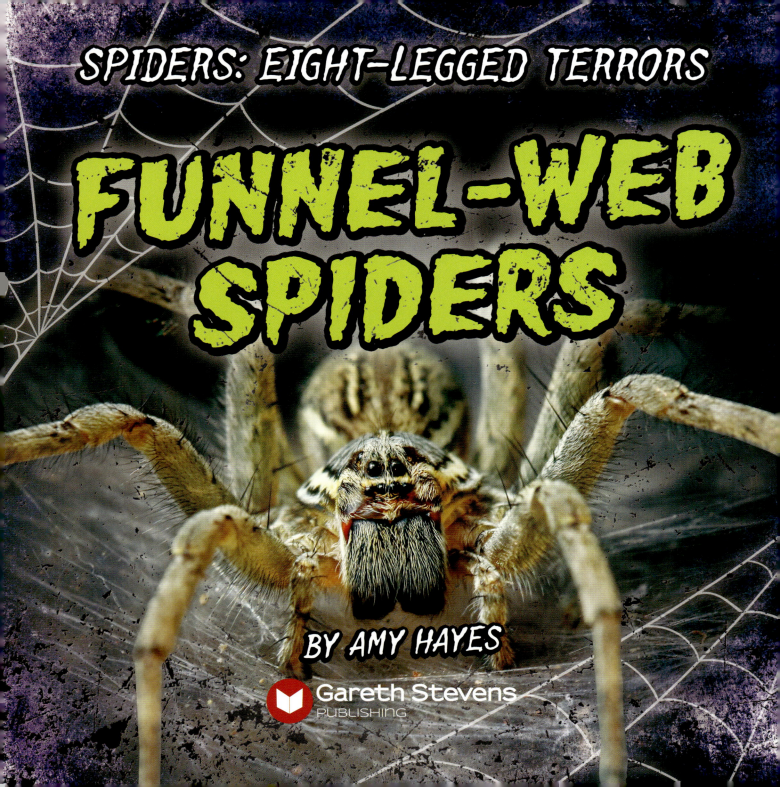

Please visit our website, www.garethstevens.com. For a free color catalog of all our high-quality books, call toll free 1-800-542-2595 or fax 1-877-542-2596.

Cataloging-in-Publication Data

Names: Hayes, Amy.
Title: Funnel-web spiders / Amy Hayes.
Description: New York : Gareth Stevens Publishing, 2018. | Series: Spiders: eight-legged terrors | Includes index.
Identifiers: ISBN 9781538202050 (pbk.) | ISBN 9781538202074 (library bound) | ISBN 9781538202067 (6 pack)
Subjects: LCSH: Agelenidae–Juvenile literature. | Funnel-web spiders.
Classification: LCC QL458.42.A3 H39 2018 | DDC 595.4'4–dc23

First Edition

Published in 2018 by
Gareth Stevens Publishing
111 East 14th Street, Suite 349
New York, NY 10003

Copyright © 2018 Gareth Stevens Publishing

Designer: Laura Bowen
Editor: Ryan Nagelhout

Photo credits: Cover, p. 1 (spider) Amith Nag Photography/Getty Images; cover, pp. 1–24 (background) Fantom666/Shutterstock.com; cover, pp. 1–24 (black splatter) Miloje/Shutterstock.com; cover, pp. 1–24 (web) Ramona Kaulitzki/Shutterstock.com; pp. 4–24 (text boxes) Tueris/Shutterstock.com; p. 5 Ken Thomas/Wikimedia Commons; p. 7 Anton Kozyrev/Shutterstock.com; p. 9 (map) Sarefo/Wikimedia Commons; p. 9 (spider) Lycaon/Wikimedia Commons; p. 11 The Sydney Morning Herald/Fairfax Media/Getty Images; p. 13 Rolf Nussbaumer/Getty Images; p. 15 Dysmachus/Wikimedia Commons; p. 17 File Upload Bot/Wikimedia Commons; p. 19 Auscape/Universal Images Group/Getty Images; p. 21 Don Johnston/Getty Images.

All rights reserved. No part of this book may be reproduced in any form without permission in writing from the publisher, except by a reviewer.

Printed in China

CPSIA compliance information: Batch #CS17GS: For further information contact Gareth Stevens, New York, New York at 1-800-542-2595.

CONTENTS

So Many Spiders 4
Funny-Shaped Webs 6
Funnel-Web Families 8
Females and Males 10
Short Lives and Sticky Webs 12
Funnel-Web Tarantulas 14
The Scariest Family 16
Most Dangerous Spider on Earth? 18
More Funnel Webs 20
Glossary 22
For More Information 23
Index 24

Words in the glossary appear in **bold** type the first time they are used in the text.

SO MANY SPIDERS

Spiders are amazing creatures. With their eight legs and—usually—eight eyes, they can be pretty scary, too! Did you know there are many different types of spiders? Perhaps you've seen a few different types outdoors or even in a dusty corner of your room.

Spiders are put into different groups. Some of the spiders are grouped because of their size. Others are grouped based on the type of webs they **weave**. One group is known as funnel-web spiders.

TERRIFYING TRUTHS

There are new types of spiders being discovered all the time! In fact, there are more than 43,000 species, or kinds, of spiders.

There are lots of different spiders all over the world, but funnel-web spiders are one of the strangest!

FUNNY-SHAPED WEBS

Have you ever seen a funnel? It's like an upside-down hollow cone—wide at the top and narrow at the bottom. Many people use a funnel in their kitchen to pour liquids.

Funnel-web spiders usually build a flat web to catch **prey** and a funnel-like tube leading to a hole where the spider hides. When something that looks good to eat—like a fly—lands on the flat web, the spider rushes out, grabs it, and returns to the funnel to eat!

TERRIFYING TRUTHS

Funnel-web spiders make **venom** that **paralyzes** prey and makes it easy for the spiders to drag them back to the center of the funnel.

Funnel webs serve as a bedroom and a kitchen for the spiders that weave them.

FUNNEL-WEB FAMILIES

Funnel-web spiders are found in many different places around the world. In fact, there are three families of funnel-web spiders: Agelenidae, which live throughout the world; Dipluridae, which live mostly in Central and South America; and Hexathelidae, which live in Australia.

Spiders in the Agelenidae family are nocturnal, which means they're active at night. You might see one in a **horizontal** funnel web in low bushes or grass. They also might make webs in the corners of homes or by sheds as well.

TERRIFYING TRUTHS

Nearly all Agelenidae spiders are harmless—we think. It is possible that the venom of the *Eratigena agrestis*, also known as the hobo spider, may be dangerous.

FEMALES AND MALES

Male funnel-web spiders don't spin webs. Instead, they wander around looking for females to **mate** with. After mating, the female will produce an egg sack. In some species, this sack is built inside the web, where baby spiders called spiderlings will live as long as 2 to 3 years before leaving to begin life on their own.

Mating is dangerous for male funnel-web spiders. After or during the mating process, the female may try to kill and eat the male spider!

TERRIFYING TRUTHS

Some male funnel-web spiders have special spurs on two of their legs to keep the females from biting them!

A scientist looking at a male Australian Sydney funnel-web spider.

For a while, people believed male funnel-web spiders had more powerful venom than females. But now it seems more likely people just meet with males (like this one) more often.

11

SHORT LIVES AND STICKY WEBS

Agelenidae spiders generally live for 1 to 2 years. Many die in the winter. But in warmer areas, they can live longer. These spiders eat a lot of bugs and other creatures—including other funnel-web spiders!

Some funnel webs are sticky. If a funnel-web spider crawls across another spider's sticky web, it can get stuck. Then it becomes spider prey! But if you see a funnel-web spider, don't be scared. It will try to stay out of your way if you stay out of its way!

TERRIFYING TRUTHS

Agelenidae spiders are some of the fastest spiders! If you surprise an Agelenidae spider, you might only catch a glance before it runs and hides.

During the 1600s and 1700s, the webs of Agelenidae spiders were used like bandages on wounds to stop bleeding.

FUNNEL-WEB TARANTULAS

Spiders in the Dipluridae family are known as funnel-web tarantulas! They're also sometimes called curtain-web spiders. Their cloudy, messy webs fill spaces under rocks, logs, and even moss. They build many funnels that reach into these spaces rather than into holes in the ground.

Unlike the other funnel-web families, Dipluridae spiders live all around the world in warm, wet **environments** such as rainforests. They also have longer **spinnerets** than many other funnel-web spiders.

TERRIFYING TRUTHS

The smallest of these spiders is only 0.12 inch (3 mm) long, but some experts say the largest can grow up to 1.2 inches (30 mm)!

See how cloudy and messy this spider's web is!

THE SCARIEST FAMILY?

Of the three funnel-web spider families, the most famous and feared is Hexathelidae. This spider family lives in Australia and is known for its powerful venom. Black or brown and somewhere between 0.3 and 2 inches (8 and 51 mm), these spiders need lots of moisture. Small but deadly, they can live up to 20 years!

Luckily for us, these spiders mostly stay in their web, except in summer, when males go out at night to search for a mate.

TERRIFYING TRUTHS

Many species of the Hexathelidae family live in burrows, or holes, with lines of silk running from them. Some species, such as *Hadronyche formidabilis*, live in trees.

Look at the silk this funnel-web spider has spun on these leaves.

MOST DANGEROUS SPIDER ON EARTH?

The Sydney funnel-web spider, or *Atrax robustus*, is considered the most dangerous spider in the world. This black or brown spider comes out after the rain, sometimes falling into swimming pools. Sometimes it will wander into homes to find a damp place to stay during the day.

If you get bitten by one of these spiders, you should get to a hospital as soon as possible! The bite will cause pain, then numbness. Scientists think you could die within a few hours of a bite!

TERRIFYING TRUTHS

Funnel-web spider bites have killed 13 people. Thankfully, there have been no deaths since the invention of a venom antidote.

Cats, dogs, and many other **mammals** are immune to the *Atrax robustus* venom. Only **primates** find their bites poisonous!

MORE FUNNEL WEBS

Funnel-web spiders are pretty amazing. Their strange webs can be found as burrows under rocks or all the way up in the treetops. Not only that, they exist all over the world! And there are many different species to learn about.

Some are mostly harmless, while others are said to be among the most feared species of spiders. While not all are deadly, it's best to leave these eight-legged terrors alone. They'll try to stay out of your way, too!

TERRIFYING TRUTHS

Funnel-web spiders are most active during wet months and summertime. Just know that they're not hunting people, so stay away, and you'll be safe and sound!

Funnel-web spiders are scary to the bugs and animals that end up as their dinner. For people, they're just an animal best left alone!

GLOSSARY

antidote: a medicine, or drug, that stops a poison from working

environment: the natural world in which an animal lives

horizontal: longer side to side, with the top and bottom on the left or right

mammal: a warm-blooded animal that has a backbone and hair, breathes air, and feeds milk to its young

mate: one of two animals that come together to produce babies; to come together to make babies

paralyze: to make unable to move

prey: an animal that is hunted by other animals for food

primate: any animal from the group that includes humans, apes, and monkeys

spinneret: the body part in a spider that makes silk

venom: something an animal makes in its body that can harm other animals

weave: to pass matter back and forth over itself to make a pattern

FOR MORE INFORMATION

BOOKS

Morgan, Sally. *Spiders*. Mankato, MN: Amicus, 2011.

Wheeler, Jill C. *Funnel-Web Spiders*. Edina, MN: ABDO Publishing, 2006.

Woolf, Alex. *Killer Spiders*. Mankato, MN: Arcturus Publishing, 2011.

WEBSITES

Family Agelenidae—Funnel Weavers
bugguide.net/node/view/1974
Find out about the funnel-web spiders in North America with this thorough guide.

Funnel-Web Spider
animalcorner.co.uk/animals/funnel-web-spider/
Learn about funnel-web spiders and other animals on this fun website.

Sydney Funnel-Web Spider
australianmuseum.net.au/sydney-funnel-web-spider
The Australian Museum has all the facts you need to know about venomous funnel-web spiders.

Publisher's note to educators and parents: Our editors have carefully reviewed these websites to ensure that they are suitable for students. Many websites change frequently, however, and we cannot guarantee that a site's future contents will continue to meet our high standards of quality and educational value. Be advised that students should be closely supervised whenever they access the Internet.

INDEX

Agelenidae 8, 9, 12, 13

Australia 8, 16

bite 18, 19

Central America 8

curtain-web spiders 14

Dipluridae 8, 9, 14

egg sack 10

eyes 4

female 10, 11

Hexathelidae 8, 9, 16

legs 4, 10

male 10, 11, 16

mate 10, 16

prey 6, 12

silk 16, 17

South America 8

species 4, 10, 16, 20

spiderlings 10

spinneret 14

venom 6, 8, 11, 16, 18, 19

webs 4, 6, 7, 8, 10, 12, 13, 14, 15, 16, 20